ZOOM IN ON

REAL-LIFE MYSTERIES

ADAPTED BY

ROSIE McCORMICK

KINGfISHER

Contents

Maybe — This might be a true story or simply a legend. Either way, it is a mystery that has not yet been scientfically explained.

False — This is a mystery that has been solved. Scientists have come up with a verifiable explanation.

Information

Anecdotes

Information

A Test

Stickers

Postcards

Old Solem

Remember your magic!

Bullit, the richest farmer on the island, placed himself squarely in front of Old Solem. Large drops of sweat were running down his face, and the little electric fan in the room barely stirred the stifling air.

"You were a great sorcerer, Solem – the greatest that our island has ever known."

"That was long ago," replied the old man. He was seated in his armchair, with one eye on the television screen.

"Solem, it has not rained for three months. It is a disaster! You must do something! You alone, the old sorcerer of the Motecks, can make it rain!" said the farmer.

"The Motecks? Rich landowners like you have stolen all our land. There are no more than about thirty of us descendants of the island tribe left. What more do you want to take from me? I have nothing left! Leave me in peace..."

"I am willing to pay you, if you can make it rain."

Old Solem looked sadly at his visitor. His hands trembled on the arms of his chair. Some people on the island of Yatag claimed that he was not quite right in the head, and that too much alcohol, too many years, had changed this wise man, once respected by everyone, into an old wreck unable to remember anything. Others said that, all right, he drank too much, but the most powerful of all the old sorcerers had not lost his gift.

"I can pay you in dollars – many dollars," said Bullit.

"Once upon a time I used to know the secret signs, the mysterious keys that opened the gates of the heavens. But now I have lost my magic and my powers."

"Find them again, and I will make you a very rich man," ordered the farmer.

"Rich?" the old man chuckled.

"Very rich, if you can make it rain."

"So what you are saying is, you can make my fortune – but you cannot make it rain?" Solem asked contemptuously.

"That's right! You will try then?"

"I will try!" the old man sighed.

"You will succeed! And by this evening! It's important – my animals and my fields both need water."

"This evening..." muttered the old man.

It is said on the island of Yatag that Old Solem did not sleep that night. People claimed they saw him put on the old headdress of the Moteck sorcerers and heard him invoke the heavens, his trembling hands raised towards the stars.

"Was it you that did it?" Bullit burst into Solem's parlour. He was beside himself, and pointed to the window. He wiped the perspiration that ran down his neck, and waited for an explanation.

"It is possible. I told you yesterday that I had forgotten the ancient spells," the old man said, without taking his eyes from the television screen.

Outside, it was impossible to see further than three metres. Since the middle of the morning, a thick fog had spread over Yatag. An unreal, mauve fog, dense as flax, which made the air even more stifling than before.

"You will try again this evening!" ordered Bullit. A wicked smile appeared on his lips. "Your house is on my land. Do not forget that I can throw you out whenever I want to."

"Is that a threat?" asked Solem.

"It's a deal. I am a businessman. This land is mine. I bought it."

"And now you want tears from heaven..."

"I want rain! I know you will succeed!" Bullit headed towards the door, adding: "I believe in your power!"

Then he went out. He did not hear Solem retort: "You are the only one who does!"

Just a question of adjustment

That very evening, in his hoarse voice, Old Solem resumed his prayers to heaven. Was it his age? Was it the effects of alcohol? A memory like a sieve? Towards the end of the night, it began to rain. But it did not rain water, which would have quenched the thirst of the ground. It was not the rain hoped for by the rich landowner. No, it began to rain petals of flowers!

Petals of roses and rhododendrons, the heads of mimosas, the tongues of tulips and a confetti of azaleas – all flowers that did not grow in the region. The air was still just as stifling, even though it was perfumed with thousands of scents. In an hour, the entire island was covered with a thick, multi-coloured mantle, as if a magical painter had played some fantastic practical joke.

"Are you trying to make a fool of me, Solem?"

Bullit tried hard to keep calm in the presence of the old man, but he felt ready to explode.

"When I put on the clothes of the ancient sorcerers of the Motecks, I never joke," Solem declared calmly, before adding: "I must have made a tiny error in pronunciation of the magic formula. It is just a question of adjustment."

"Well," said Bullit, brushing away some marguerite petals from his hair, "it's true it has rained something, but my lands and my herds need water, not this kind of rubbish. Is that quite clear, you old madman?" Bullit thumped the television. "Do you want me to throw you out onto the street?"

"I am tired," said the old man. "With everything that's happened, I haven't slept for two nights."

"Solem, your third attempt will be the last – and the one that succeeds!"

"I am tired, I tell you!" The old man seized hold of the television's remote control and, without looking at Bullit, punched the buttons to find a programme.

"You are the greatest sorcerer left. You must succeed!" Bullit repeated firmly. He turned the armchair round and brought out a wad of dollars from one of the pockets in his shirt. He

put them on top of the television. "There will be three times this amount for you if you can make it rain as early as tomorrow. If not..."

"You possess two-thirds of anything that grazes on four feet on this island, more than half the land of Yatag belongs to you, our houses too.. But you also want the sky, the rays of the Sun, the clouds – everything!"

"Yes, that's right. I want everything, and more besides," replied Bullit, amused.

"It will rain tomorrow. Now get out and leave me in peace!"

There you are, it's done!

That night, so they say, the wind got up in no time at all and swept away the perfumed carpet of dried petals that covered the entire island. Old Solem, wearing the attire of the Moteck sorcerers, seemed satisfied as he looked at the thick black clouds masking the Moon and stars. He breathed deeply before continuing with the dance of his ancestors.

For a long time his rough voice accompanied the wind blowing. The song sounded strange and false, but possessed an undeniable power. The steps of the dance seemed clumsy, but he repeated them for more than an hour without

leaving the circle of ash that he had traced on the ground. Sometimes he stopped, perhaps searching for the right words, perhaps simply to appreciate the change that was taking place above him.

Again and again, Old Solem chanted to the heavens and executed his clumsy dance. He became exhausted, going round and round in the circle, lifting his arms upwards. But nothing could stop him. And when the first drop of water splashed down into the circle of ash, Old Solem was at last able to stop the ceremony and go home to sleep.

It was the first great raindrop of what became a torrent. It arrived like a scout ahead of an army of voluminous drops which, in only a few seconds, supported by a battery of lightning, attacked the entire island of Yatag.

A deluge.

Towards the end of the afternoon, Bullit arrived soaked to the skin. He entered Old Solem's house without knocking.

"I knew that I could count on you! I have come to pay you what I promised," he said happily, advancing towards the armchair with a huge wad of notes in his hand. "You made this storm continue for nearly a week, and that's okay. But now you must stop the storm for me, because I need to get in the harvest."

He did not realize at first that the old man was

dead. Solem seemed to be dozing, his head resting slightly to one side, a smile hovering on his lips. Bullit put the money back in his pocket, and took back the wad he had placed on top of the television the previous day. He thought that he had done excellent business. What a bargain!

Two months later, Bullit was still asking with great anguish, when the terrible downpour would cease.

Inhabitants of the Night

At night, when it's dark and the wind is howling, it is easy to imagine that many night-time sounds and shadows are actually ghosts!

Was it a ghost?

Throughout history, people have claimed to see ghosts. They have often described them as hovering, transparent shapes resembling a human form. Some have even claimed to see ghosts in the form of ferocious beasts. Others have felt rather than seen a cold, foreboding presence.

A screech owl is a nocturnal bird of prey.

Night-time screams

The sound of a lonesome creature, crying or screeching into the night, is enough to trigger most people's imagination. That is why the *screech owl* is probably responsible for many a tall tale told late at night beside a flickering fire. Its cry has been mistaken for the sound of rattling chains. And with its white-feathered wings gliding across a moonlit sky, it has probably unnerved even the most determined sceptics.

Forest dwellers

It has always been easy to imagine ghouls and goblins in dark, inhospitable environments. In days gone by, unexplored forests were thought to be suitable dwelling

places for all kinds of creatures. Dragons, gnomes, goblins, elves and sprites were ready to pounce on any unsuspecting human.

Night lights

Many a traveller wandering home at night from a nearby town or village has reported seeing a sudden spark of light burst up from the dark earth. This isn't really a mystery at all, just a chemical reaction. In marsh or bogland areas, decaying matter such as rotting leaves and root, give off methane gas that can spontaneously ignite and produce small, bluish flames.

Werewolves

Bizarre tales about werewolves are popular throughout the world. People are transformed into ferocious hairy beasts by the power of a full Moon, and they prey upon the innocent and pure. Once the wolf has taken over the man, he cannot change back.

How to See a Ghost

Stare at the black image of the ghost below for 30 seconds, then look at the stone archway. The shadow of the ghost should appear in the archway.

Optical illusions

Obviously, you haven't seen a ghost but an optical illusion. This occurred because the retina, the part of your eye on which an image is formed, was tricked. First it focused on a solid dark image, but then it had to switch suddenly and take in an entirely white surface. Having to cope with both a black and a white image caused retinal signals, or messages, to the brain to become confused, and the result was a greyish image floating in the stone doorway.

Mixed messages

Here are three illusions. First, which is bigger, the black square in the white box, or the white square in the black box? Or are they the same size? Next, which colours are darker, the coloured squares in the white block, or the coloured squares in the black block? Or are they the same? Finally, can you see grey dots in the white lines between the blue squares? These three illusions are created by your brain as it analyzes the images side by side.

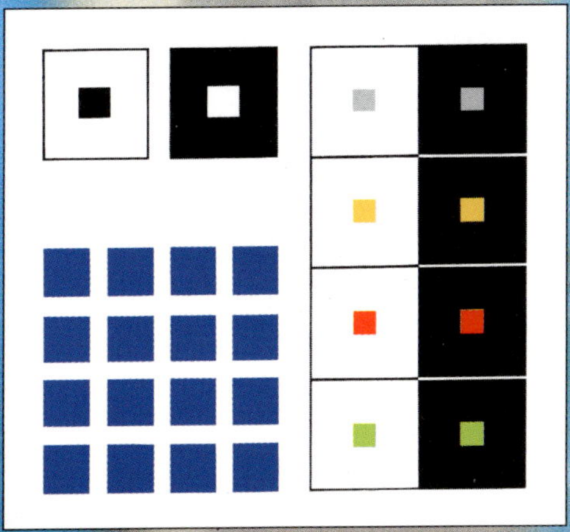

Mirages

What do you call it when a tar-surfaced road suddenly becomes a shimmering stream, or a sand-dune a shady oasis?

Ship ahoy!

Mirages can occur at sea as well. But because air is colder on the surface of the sea, and warmer higher up, light rays are bent not upwards but downwards. This could explain the many tales sailors have told of a mysterious 'flying' ship, seen floating above the horizon.

Mirage magic

You call it a mirage, that's what! Mirages occur when light, which normally travels through the air in a straight line, follows a curved line instead. Mirages are more common in hot places such as deserts, because the air near the ground is warmer than the air higher up. As a result, the warmer air acts like a magnifying glass and distorts, or bends, light rays upwards. So your eyes are being tricked!

The Flying Dutchman

In 1650, a Dutch merchant ship called the *Bintang* set sail from Holland for Indonesia on Good Friday. It never reached its final destination. It was supposedly spotted one year later by another Dutch ship in the Indian Ocean. The crew claimed that as they approached the vessel, it simply vanished into thin air. And so began the legend of the Flying Dutchman.

Light beams in space

In space, light beams can also be distorted when passing close to clusters of stars. The light beam is literally steered off-course by the force of gravity.

Is There a Monster

Loch Ness is a deep lake in the Scottish Highlands. It holds three times more water than any other lake in Britain. Enough to hide a giant monster, perhaps?

A tale from long ago

Reports of the *Loch* Ness monster go back to AD 563 when St Columba, the abbot of Iona, supposedly saved a monk called Lugne from being devoured by the beast. 'Nessie' had already mauled one victim. St Columba demanded, in the name of God, that the beast retreat into the watery depths and leave the poor monk alone. Nessie did just that, and the monk was saved.

Loch is the Scottish word for a lake situated in a valley.

A plesiosaur was a marine reptile of the Mesozoic era.

Searching for the truth

In 1934, naval officer Rupert Gould published the first book about Nessie. He proposed that large sea animals, such as *plesiosaurs*, arrived in Loch Ness thousands of years ago when the loch was joined to the sea. As the coastline changed, they became cut off from the sea, and the loch became a permanent home.

in Loch Ness?

Eyewitness accounts

There has been a lot of interest in Nessie and thousands of sightings since Gould first published his book. Many blurred black-and-white photographs have been offered up as evidence. The first colour photograph was taken in 1977 by a man standing in the grounds of a nearby castle. However, there is still no solid proof that the elusive beast does exist.

Loch Ness facts

Six rivers flow into Loch Ness, but only one (the river Ness) flows out. The loch is 36 km long, and over one third of it is deeper than 200 m – which is more than twice the depth of the North Sea. Deep enough for a monster?

Yeti and Bigfoot

Most of the world has been explored, but there are still some remote, uninhabited places where few people venture – that's where stories of large, hairy beasts emerge.

A humanoid is a creature that looks like a human being.

Neandertals were early humans who lived in Palaeolithic times about 30,000 years ago. Their remains were found in a cave in the Neandertal Valley.

Ancient man

It is hard to believe that a small number of our very distant ancestors, known as *Neandertals*, have survived unchanged since prehistoric times. But this is how some people explained the strange stories of large, hairy *humanoids* that first emerged from remote wooded areas of the northwest United States and Canada. A creature standing three metres tall left behind a trail of enormous footprints.

Bigfoot on film

In recent times this giant, elusive creature has been nicknamed Bigfoot. In 1967 at Bluff Creek, California, two men called Roger Patterson and Bob Gimlin claim to have come across Bigfoot as it crouched beside a stream. Startled by the men, it ran off into the woods – but not before Roger Patterson had taken a photograph. It has never been satisfactorily proved whether or not the photograph is a fake.

The Yeti

In 1921, a group of climbers led by a British army colonel set off into the treacherous Himalayan mountains. Suddenly, they spotted some shadowy figures moving across a snowfield just above them. When they reached the spot, they discovered a trail of enormous foot prints. Local sherpas told them they had been made by a legendary creature known as Metoh Kangmi. Today it is widely referred to as a Yeti.

The mystery hunt

Cryptozoology is the science that studies strange and unknown creatures, such as the Loch Ness Monster, Big Foot and the Yeti. Cryptozoologists follow the principle that at the heart of every fairy tale there might be a grain of truth. And so they search for clues, interview witnesses, study the evidence and attempt to uncover the 'real' facts.

Vampires

From every corner of the world come strange stories about vampires – people or batlike creatures that drink blood.

Vlad the Impaler

Perhaps the most famous of these tales comes from Transylvania, a province in Romania. This is the setting for Bram Stoker's 1897 novel, *Dracula*. The story is supposedly based on a real-life, blood-thirsty noble called Vlad IV of Wallachia (*c.*1431–1476). Vlad enjoyed inflicting pain on his enemies – he impaled hundreds of them on sharp stakes.

How to recognize a vampire

Vampires have no reflection and they cannot tolerate sunlight or crucifixes. If you want to know how to get rid of one, here's how to do it!

1. Drive a hawthorn stake through its heart.
2. Place small stones inside the vampire's coffin.
3. Bury the vampire face-down in its coffin.
4. Surround yourself and the vampire with fresh garlic.
5. Scatter millet seeds over its body.
6. Place wild, thorny roses just outside its coffin.

Mrs Vampire

A Hungarian noblewoman called Elizabeth Bathroy (*c.*1560–1614) certainly rivalled Vlad IV when it came to satisfying a thirst for blood. She believed that if she drank enough human blood, and bathed in it too, it would keep her young forever. She is supposed to have been responsible for the deaths of almost 700 people.

The real thing

The South American vampire bat feeds on animal blood. It bites the skin of its victim with its sharp, fanglike teeth, and anaesthetizes the animal with its saliva. Then, undisturbed, it settles down to a bloody feast.

For thousands of years, people have gazed in awe at the Moon. And even though astronauts have now landed on its surface, its powers are still a mystery.

The Moon washes whiter

Before the invention of the washing machine and modern washing powders, our ancestors laid their laundry out on the ground at night beneath a full Moon. They believed that the Moon revived the fading fabric and made it whiter. Today, scientists agree that this is possible, due to a chemical reaction. Beneath a full Moon and cloudless sky, ozone and water vapour mix together to produce hydrogen peroxide – a natural bleach, created by the power of nature!

The Effects of the Full Moon

Rising tides

It is not true that the Moon can make your hair – or carrots – grow. But it is responsible for the regular rise and fall of water in the oceans. Tides are caused by the Moon's gravity pulling the water towards it.

High tides occur when the Earth, Moon and Sun are in perfect alignment, and the Sun's gravity is added to the Moon's.

Moon myths

In many parts of the world, the Moon was traditionally regarded as a symbol of fertility. Long ago, in Arctic lands, young girls were afraid to look at the Moon in case they became pregnant. And in Breton, in northwest France, women once believed that if they exposed their bodies to the moonlight, they would give birth to monsters.

Silence – we're rolling!

This isn't a haunted house, just a filmset. Yet things are not what they seem. Look closely at the picture – there are 22 mistakes. Can you spot them?

Solution on p.63

Astrology –

Astrologers study the movements of the Sun, Moon, planets and stars. They say that people's lives are shaped by the position of the heavens at their birth.

Studying the stars

Ancient cultures studied the night sky, searching for information about the world. But over time, the study of the Universe became a more accurate science. *Astronomers* questioned the views held by the *astrologers*.

Astrologers claim to forecast our future by looking at the heavenly bodies.

Astronomers are scientists who study the planets and the Universe.

Fact or Fiction?

A constellation is any one of the 88 groups of stars named by the Ancient Greeks.

Room for error

In 1610, Galileo used a telescope to study the planets, and astronomy and astrology moved even further apart. Astronomers gained scientific knowledge and dismissed astrology as fiction. There certainly are discrepancies:

- The galaxies are made up of billions of stars. Why is it that only some of these influence our destiny?
- The astrologers' constellations group stars that, from an astronomer's point of view, have no connection at all.
- Over time, the constellations have drifted to such an extent that they no longer resemble their original form.
- Astrological predictions are made from stars in the Northern Hemisphere. How are predictions made for people living in other parts of the world?

Modern religion

Even though astrology is not an exact science, many people do believe in it. They read their horoscope each day and use it to guide them in their daily lives. If astrology offers a sense of wellbeing, or even appears to answer certain questions, then perhaps it does have some relevance!

The Power

Are our minds more powerful than we realize? Do we have the ability to read minds, or even move objects from place to place? Some people believe we do!

This is magic!

Magicians use illusion to make us believe that they can read minds, make objects suddenly become mobile, and even levitate people. They employ age-old secrets and tricks of the trade. But even though we know this, their tricks still capture our imagination.

The paranormal is beyond explanation.

Remote viewing

Some people do appear to have *paranormal* powers that cannot be explained. A New York artist called Ingo Swann appears to be able to do the impossible. In controlled conditions at Stanford Research Institute, California, Swann showed he could 'see' events many kilometres away.

Information of the Mind

The Rhine frauds

In the 1960s, Joseph Rhine conducted extrasensory perception (*ESP*) tests.

In these tests, people claimed they could guess the content of hidden drawings. Some of the tests were successful, but others were not. Rhine was so convinced of the existence of ESP and the powers of telepathy that he altered the less favourable results, making the entire experiment a fraud.

ESP is the ability to get information without the use of the normal senses.

Psychic predicts crash

In October 1930, a psychic called Alice Garnett predicted that the newly-developed giant airship, the R101, would crash. Days after she announced her premonition to the press, the R101 did indeed crash. It came down over France while on its maiden flight from England to India. Alice claimed that the dead pilot, Lieutenant Carmichael Irwin, had made contact with her to explain the cause of the crash. According to Alice, the pilot told her that the airship should never have flown. It was much too heavy for its engines. He claimed that the British government knew this but wanted to go ahead anyway. Years later, government papers confirmed Alice's story.

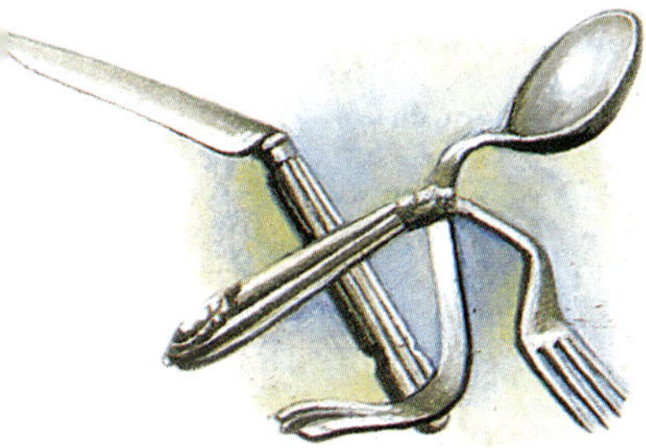

Dowsers and

Finding an underground spring with a simple rod may seem impossible, but there is some proof that it actually works!

Gone dowsing!

People who search for underground water and minerals are called dowsers. Traditionally they use a forked hazel twig called a divining rod. The twig moves, or dips, above the exact spot.

The Earth's magnetic field is a natural phenomenon that makes compass needles point north.

How do they do that?

Geologists have a theory as to why dowsers appear to be successful. Subterranean rivers and metal deposits may affect the Earth's *magnetic field*. Because of the presence of iron ore, known as *magnetite*, in the human body, a minute magnetic reaction occurs. This reaction causes an involuntary movement of the dowser's muscles – and a sudden movement of the divining rod.

Water-witching

In the United States, dowsing is sometimes referred to as water-witching. Some dowsers can detect not only where underground water supplies can be found, but also how far down the water is and how much of it there is!

Magnetite is a dark, dense mineral that has very strong magnetism.

Divining Rods

We need water

One of the most successful water dowsers is a Californian called Jack Livingstone. During a period of drought in 1976 to 1977, he managed to pinpoint a number of underground water supplies. His most famous find was an underground spring in a public park. Not only did he find it, but he accurately predicted that the spring would yield about 680 litres of water per minute.

The Mysteries

India appears to have its own special kind of magic – from snake charmers to those who can recline on a bed of nails.

Snake charmers

Can a snake charmer really hypnotize a deadly cobra with the sound of his flute? The answer is 'no', because snakes are deaf. What the snake is really reacting to, as it emerges from the charmer's bag of tricks, is the movement of the flute from side to side. And, as a precautionary measure, snake charmers usually remove the snake's poison.

Land of the guru

There are many gurus, or spiritual leaders, in India. Perhaps one of the most famous is Sai Baba. He is known for his apparent healing powers and for his ability to pluck objects on demand out of thin air. For over 50 years, Sai Baba has been demonstrating his extraordinary powers. So far, no one has discovered any evidence of trickery.

Information

of India

The bed of nails

The ability to sit on a bed of nails without turning into a human pin-cushion is not really magic, but science. If the nails are sufficiently close together, the weight of the body is safely spread over numerous points. Even so, it is extremely uncomfortable.

The magic rope

Many travellers have stood in a hot and dusty Indian marketplace and watched what appears to be magic. A rope rises up into the air and then a boy climbs to the top of it. But a rope cannot rise up into the air simply because someone asks it to. If you want to know how it is done, read on... The magician sits on a grill covering a well. His accomplices in the well hold up a bamboo pole covered in rope. They hold it steady as the boy climbs to the top.

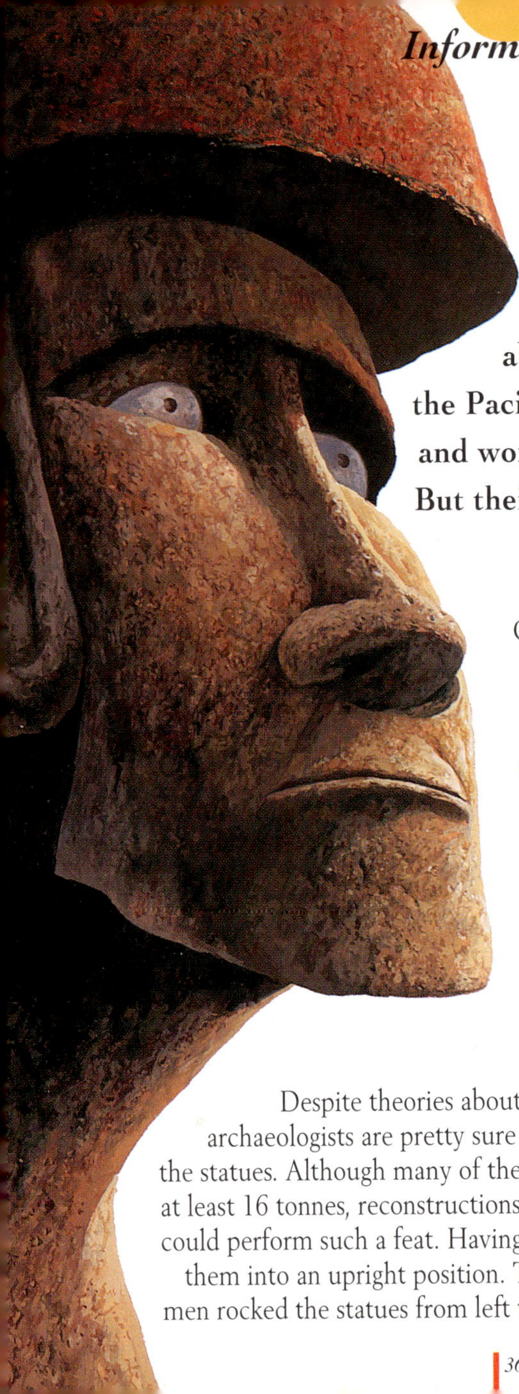

The Easter

Giant statues of strange beings stand alone and abandoned on a small island in the Pacific Ocean. They are battered and worn by the winds and by time. But their origin can be explained.

Stone giants

On Easter Sunday in 1722, a Dutchman called Roggeveen came upon the island of Rapa Nui. Now known as Easter Island, it lies 4,000 km off the coast of Chile. To Roggeveen's great surprise, he found hundreds of monoliths (large blocks of stone), staring ominously out to sea. There have been dozens of theories about who or what placed them there. But there is a fairly simple explanation.

Aliens at work?

Despite theories about aliens placing the statues on the island, archaeologists are pretty sure that native islanders carved and erected the statues. Although many of them stand over ten metres tall, and weigh at least 16 tonnes, reconstructions of the task have proved that man alone could perform such a feat. Having carved the stones, the islanders levered them into an upright position. Then, with the aid of ropes, hundreds of men rocked the statues from left to right towards their final resting place.

Island Statues

The long ears versus the short ears

Over the years, islanders told archaeologists stories about their history. Thanks to this oral tradition, we have been able to learn much about the statues. The island had a history of war between two distinct tribes of people – those with long ears and those with short ears. The long ears were the descendants of the old ruling race – and it is their features that are depicted in the statues.

Islanders with bright red hair

Many of the statues appear to be wearing a red stone headdress called *pukao* (topknot) – many of the original islanders had bright red hair. The statues were carved over a period of many years. Carbon dating has revealed that the last of the statues were carved around 1680. Perhaps they were used for worship, since more than 200 altars still stand along the coast.

The Nazca Drawings

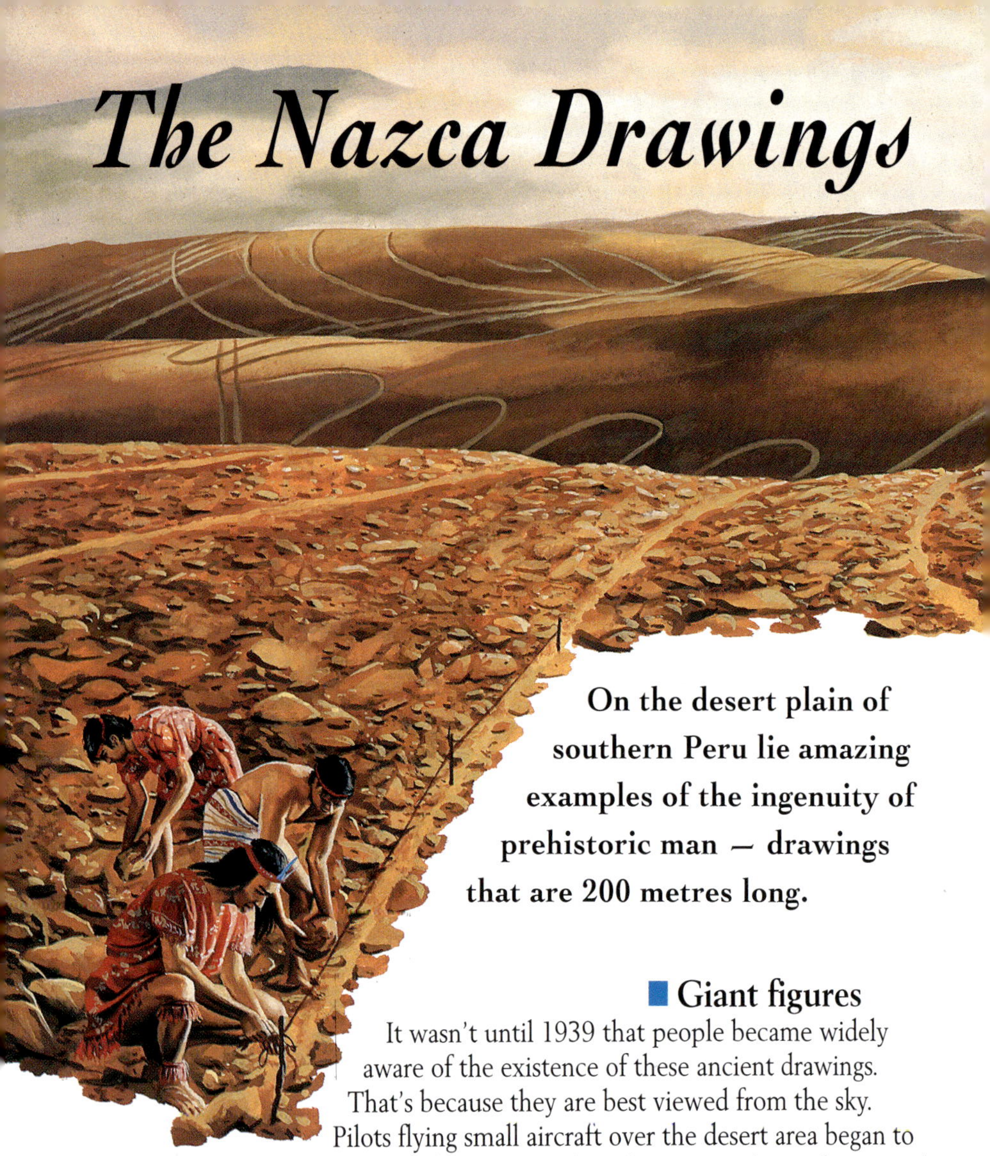

On the desert plain of southern Peru lie amazing examples of the ingenuity of prehistoric man – drawings that are 200 metres long.

Giant figures

It wasn't until 1939 that people became widely aware of the existence of these ancient drawings. That's because they are best viewed from the sky. Pilots flying small aircraft over the desert area began to make reports about unusual markings carved into the ground below. Archaeologists have since discovered that many of the drawings are of animals. They may have been tribal totems, a sign for the gods, or sacred paths trod by priests.

How did they do that?

The Paracas and Nazca Indians living in this region of Peru between 200 BC and AD 600 were skilful potters and weavers. But how did they achieve such highly complex drawings, when it is impossible to view the figures from the ground? Some people believe that they began by making scaled-down drawings. They then used ropes and *stone stakes* to map out the figure.

Could these early peoples fly?

Bill Spohrer, a member of the International Explorer's Society, set out to prove that these early peoples had discovered how to fly. His theory began when he unearthed pieces of early pottery that contained pictures of hot-air balloons and kites, as well as fabrics lighter than modern-day parachute material. In November 1975, he put his theory to the test. Using only materials available to the ancient Nazca and Paracas Indians, he took to the sky in a home-made hot-air balloon.

Stone stakes, or markers, have been found by archaeologists on the Nazca plateau.

Anamorphosis

At a certain angle, incomprehensible drawings suddenly seem to make sense.

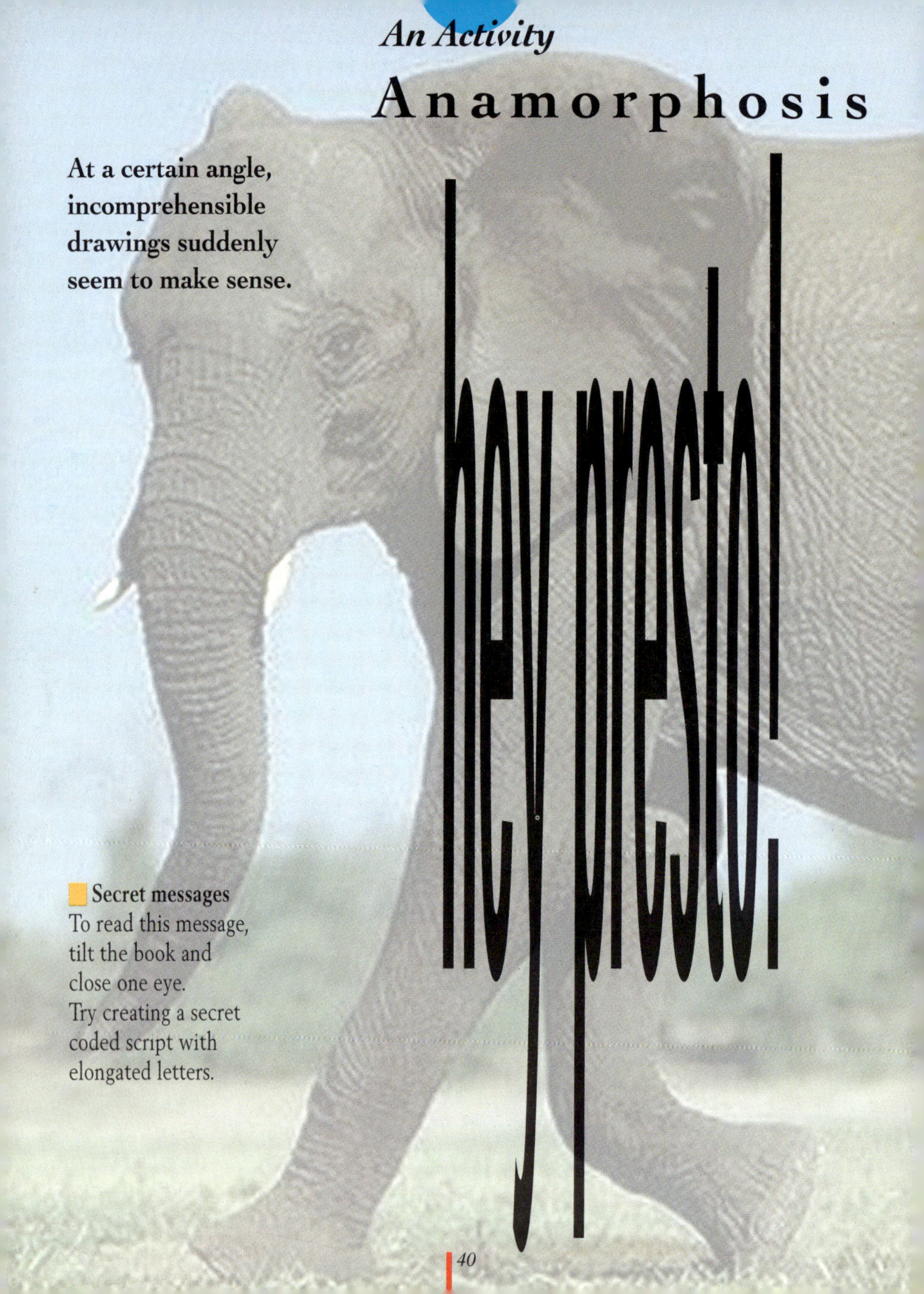

Secret messages

To read this message, tilt the book and close one eye.
Try creating a secret coded script with elongated letters.

How to create your own anamorphosis

1. Draw a grid for a normal drawing.

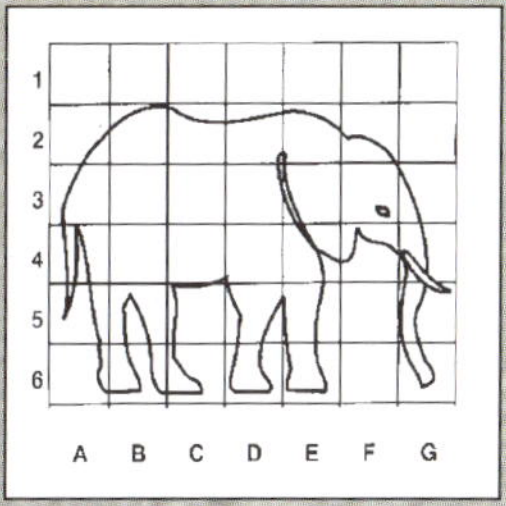

2. Draw a grid three times as long, and then copy your drawing. You can see the distorted drawing as it really should be by tilting the paper and holding it a few centimetres away from your eye.

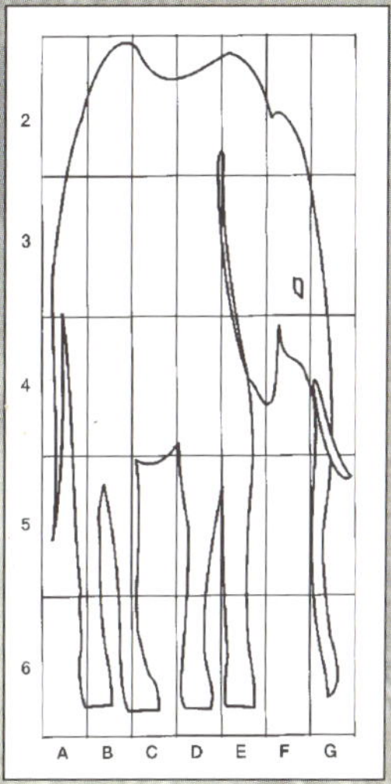

Megaliths

Giant standing stones, called megaliths, rise up from the misty moors and plains of Europe. They are messages from our *Neolithic* ancestors. But what do they mean?

Neolithic refers to the Stone Age between 5000 and 2000BC.

Mysterious standing stones

Standing stones are large, oblong stones placed on the ground in an upright position. Many sites contain stones arranged in a series of parallel lines. At Erdeven in Brittany, France, there are ten rows of stones. Each row is 2,105 m long,

Stone circles

A circle of prehistoric standing stones is called a cromlech. Perhaps the most famous example of a cromlech is Stonehenge, in England. Stonehenge provides us with clues to the world our ancestors inhabited. The stones were not randomly placed. Particular stones are aligned to the sunrise, and to the position of the Moon and stars.

Dolmens

Dolmens consist of a flat stone, weighing several tonnes, placed on top of two or three standing stones. Legend has it that fairies came to dance around them, or that human sacrifices were carried out beneath them. In fact, they were originally covered with earth to form a burial chamber. We know this because archaeologists have unearthed human bones, weapons and precious stones.

A well-organized society

A great deal of time, manpower and planning was required to erect these megaliths. With ropes, wooden rollers and hundreds of men, many of the stones were pulled hundreds of kilometres from the quarries and then hauled into position. Some of the sites were completed in phases, with each generation carrying on the work their parents or grandparents had started. Stonehenge was built in three phases. The first phase began around 2500 BC, the final phase about 1,000 years later.

Stonehenge

The Pharaoh's

For thousands of years, the mummy of Tutankhamun lay undisturbed. Did those who ventured into the sacred tomb become victims of an ancient curse?

The curse

For much of his life, Howard Carter searched for Tutankhamun's tomb in the Valley of the Kings. On November 26, 1922 Carter and his patron Lord Carnarvon found it. The tomb was excavated and the pharaoh's mummy was removed. Afterwards, some of the people involved in the excavation died. Inscribed on a stone tablet beside the pharaoh's body were the words: 'Death will slay with his wings whoever disturbs the peace of the Pharaoh'.

What really killed them?

Lord Carnarvon died some five months later and, as the months and years passed, others died too. Although it might be tempting to believe that the curse actually worked, evidence suggests that some of these deaths have a more scientific explanation. It would appear that, at the time of the excavation, the tunnels inside the pyramids were inhabited by bats. Growing in their excrement were microscopic mushrooms that gave off a sometimes deadly gas.

Curse

A strange coincidence

In 1982, a survivor of the expedition, Richard Adamson, announced that the curse had been invented by the excavation team to keep people away from the site. Even so, there is one story that seems hard to explain. While Carnarvon was working on the excavation he was bitten on the face by a mosquito. It is unclear whether or not this caused his death. However, when the body of Tutankhamun was examined by archaeologists, he too had a mark in exactly the same spot on his face!

Incredible

TEASPOONS AND CHAMPAGNE

Some people believe that inserting a small teaspoon into the neck of an opened bottle of champagne preserves the gas in the liquid. But tests carried out by the Inter-Professional Champagne Committee have challenged this view. The committee carried out tests on dozens of bottles of uncorked champagne. They measured the rate at which the carbon dioxide disappeared, both with and without a teaspoon, and came to the conclusion that a teaspoon did not slow down the process.

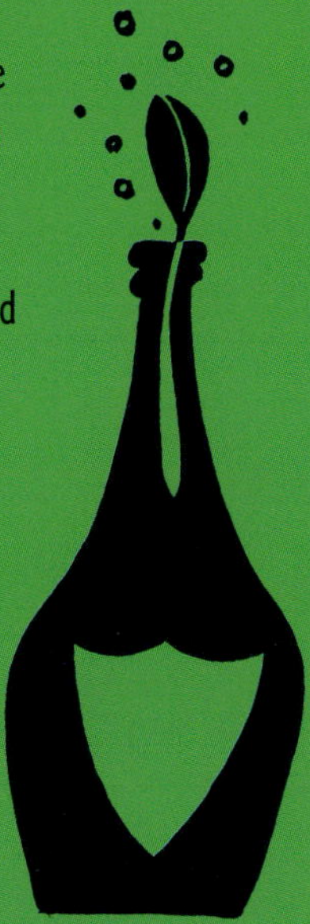

WHIRLPOOL IN THE WASHBASIN

Have you noticed that as a washbasin empties, a whirlpool of water always swirls round and round in the same direction? This natural phenomenon, known as the Coriolis effect, is caused by the Earth's rotation. As the Earth rotates, it carries with it masses of air and water. In the Northern Hemisphere the water swirls about in an anti-clockwise direction, and in the Southern Hemisphere it goes the other way.

but True!

THE COTTINGLEY FAIRIES

For thousands of years, people have imagined the existence of fairies. One day in 1917, two young English girls claimed to have taken photographs of them. They showed the photographs to their families and friends, who all agreed that the images of the fairies were incredible. Many years later, they admitted that they had staged the whole thing. They had placed cardboard cut-outs of fairies in the wood and photographed them.

RAINING FROGS

Yes, it is true that it can rain frogs! But the frogs do not originate in the sky. They are scooped up from their watery homes by fierce tornadoes, and then deposited elsewhere.

The Lost Continent

A lost civilization, once prosperous and fair, is now lost to us forever. This is the enduring story of Atlantis. No one knows for sure whether Atlantis ever actually existed.

How the legend first began

The first written account of Atlantis comes from the Greek philosopher Plato in 355 BC. He placed this civilization some 11,500 years ago, on an island in the Atlantic opposite the *Straits of Gibraltar*.

The Straits of Gibraltar are the sea between Spain and Morocco.

# of Atlantis

A myth is an ancient traditional story that explains natural events or phenomenon by introducing imaginary characters.

A scientific theory: Santorini island

Plato placed Atlantis near Gibraltar, but scientists have investigated volcanic ash around the island of Crete. Their research reveals that a huge volcanic eruption occurred on the nearby island of Santorini around 1400 BC. Is the *myth* of Atlantis actually the story of this catastrophe?

The Atlantics were the inhabitants of Atlantis.

Utopia: the perfect world

In his story about the *Atlantics,* Plato described a perfect world – a society run by the good and the wise – that was eventually swallowed up by the sea. Although much of Plato's account is thought to be a myth, rather than the truth, some historians believe that Plato was drawing upon existing stories, handed down by word of mouth.

A legendary source of inspiration

Perhaps it doesn't really matter whether or not Atlantis really existed. The story that Plato told is still a powerful one. For hundreds of years it has inspired writers, artists and philosophers to allow their imaginations to take flight. And it has served as a warning to all societies that human aggression can be the downfall of even the most perfect of worlds.

The Bermuda Triangle

Between Florida, Bermuda and Puerto Rico is a vast area of sea and sky. Known as the Bermuda Triangle, it has been the site of many mysterious disappearances.

Missing aeroplanes and ships

Stories about strange occurrences in the western Atlantic go back hundreds of years. In fact Christopher Columbus recorded that while sailing through the Sargasso Sea in 1492, his compass needle pointed northwest instead of north. In more recent times, dozens of planes and ships have vanished, never to be seen or heard of again. In 1918 the USS *Cyclops* completely disappeared, along with its entire crew, in calm water while en route to Baltimore from Barbados. At the time, it was the largest ship in the US navy to disappear without trace.

Flight 19

In December 1945, a squadron of US planes set out from a Florida naval air station on a routine mission. Hours later, a radio tower picked up a conversation between the pilots that revealed that they were lost. Attempts were made to guide them back to base. But the pilots could not pinpoint their location and eventually all contact was lost – forever!

The case of the missing tanker

On December 30, 1976 an enormous oil tanker called the *Grand Zenith* reported bad weather conditions in the Atlantic. Soon afterwards, all contact with the ship was lost. Search vessels and aircraft were sent out to assist her, but the ship was nowhere to be seen. A huge tanker carrying over thirty million litres of oil had completely disappeared.

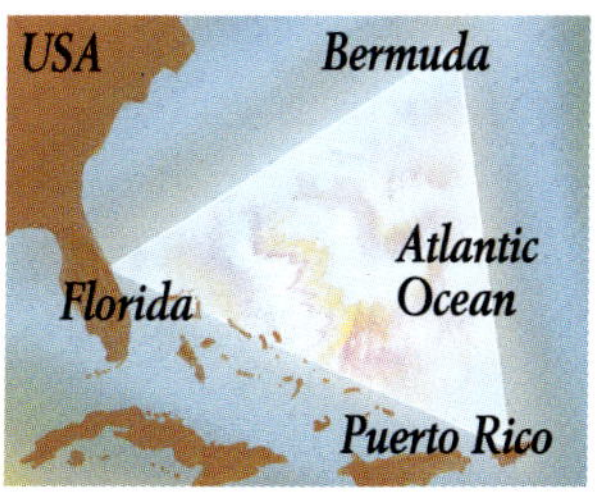

Solving the mystery

In an attempt to solve the mystery of the Bermuda Triangle, several theories have been put forward. The most popular are perhaps the most likely. Some scientists believe that a significant magnetic anomaly in the region distorts the navigational equipment of aeroplanes and ships. That, combined with strong Gulf Stream currents and bad weather conditions, has made this part of the Atlantic a treacherous place.

Rumours: are

Rumours, sometimes based on a grain of truth, spread like wildfire, and soon no one can tell what is fact and what is fiction.

Reliable sources?

Rumours are spread in various ways and are exaggerated with each retelling. Sometimes we may misinterpret a newspaper article. Occasionally, when someone tells us a story, we 'read between the lines' and come up with our own version of the events described.

The origin of the tale

Sociologists have attempted to trace various modern myths to their original source. This has proved virtually impossible, as everyone questioned refers to someone else as the instigator of the tale.

they Modern Fairytales?

Tall tales

- A woman accidentally swallowed a tadpole.
Later, while undergoing an operation, a frog jumped out of her stomach.
- Alligators have made the New York City sewers their home.
- A driver once picked up a female hitch-hiker. They talked for a while but then, to the driver's amazement, the girl vanished into thin air. He rushed to the police station to report the incident. The police informed him that a young girl was killed in a car accident at the place where he first encountered her.

Urban myths

Now that most of the population live in towns and cities, one no longer hears stories about wolves howling beneath a moonlit sky, or elves dancing in the wooded glades. Today, our imagination is fuelled by stories of aliens from outer space.

Flying Saucers

Are there really such things as flying saucers? Some people believe there are, because they claim to have seen them.

Flying saucers are also known as unidentified flying objects (UFOs).

On a bright summer's day
It all began on June 24, 1947. Kenneth Arnold was flying his private plane over Mount Rainier in Washington State and caught sight of six flat, luminous discs whizzing across the sky. He said it was like watching saucers skimming across water – and so the term *flying saucer* was born. Since then, thousands of people from every corner of the Earth have reported seeing strange shapes and lights in the sky.

Alien encounters
Often these sightings are optical illusions or have other, quite rational explanations. Clouds, aeroplanes and weather balloons have been mistaken for UFOs, as have fragments of satellites that fall to Earth. Some people claim to have seen not just UFOs, but aliens as well. And there are even those who have gone so far as to claim that they have been kidnapped and taken on board alien spaceships!

Are we alone?
As verbal reports alone do not count as evidence, we do not know whether or not there is life on other planets, or whether we have been visited by extraterrestrials. But it is possible to imagine that somewhere in the great Universe, there are other life forms besides the ones that exist on our planet.

Listening to the stars

On Earth, we can pick up a large number of electronic signals coming from space. Radio waves carry the signals and change them into sounds that we can hear. Despite careful monitoring of these signals, no intelligible message has been detected as yet. But NASA has used the *Voyager 2* probe to transport messages from people on Earth up into space.

ET – Green or Grey?

Are there aliens out there, somewhere in space, watching us? Perhaps there are aliens in our midst and we don't even know it! What would people really do if aliens arrived on Earth? Well, you might just be surprised!

The war of the worlds did not take place

On October 30, 1938 US radio broadcast a breathless report: "Flying saucers are landing in New York and Martians are stepping out of them." Almost two million listeners panicked and attempted to flee the city. Long traffic jams and widespread pandemonium were the result of a practical joke carried out by the actor and director Orson Welles. He had been reading H G Wells's science fiction novel, *The War of the Worlds.*

The Roswell incident

In 1947, staff at a US military base in the New Mexico desert made an extraordinary announcement. They claimed to be in possession of a spacecraft that had crashed to Earth. Hours later they announced that they had made a mistake – it was really a weather balloon. The plot thickened as curious reporters were warned off the story, and military staff were ordered not to talk. Since then, eyewitnesses have come forward to claim that there was a spacecraft, and alien bodies too!

An unidentifiable flying object?

In July 1969, the crew of Apollo 11 reported seeing lights coming from a UFO. Ground control said it was probably space junk. But after the rocket had landed on the Moon the lights appeared again. This time they were coming from the Moon's surface!

True o

Myths are ancient religions.

False. Myths explain natural events through the involvement of gods or imaginary characters.

You can see lovely mirages in the Gobi Desert.

False. The Gobi is a cold desert. A mirage can only appear if the air close to the ground is very hot.

In the Middle Ages, they burned cats and witches.

True. Certain women were sometimes accused of witchcraft. After a quick trial, they were burned - as were black cats - in a public place.

Some metals can spontaneously bend under the action of heat.

True. Some alloys have the ability to revert to their original form when they are reheated. This is a spectacular but scientific phenomenon.

False?

The ancients used magic to move huge blocks of stone.

False. They only had their arms and some tools, but they combined the efforts in order to carry heavy stones over great distances.

Plants can feel human emotions.

False. This is just a rumour, although some plants, like the Venus fly-trap, seem almost human in their behaviour.

There are other planets like Earth.

Perhaps. Astronomers are searching the cosmos for signs of planets turning around their own sun. What a stroke of luck if the Earth had a twin! But Earth is the only known planet with life – so far.

Planet Mars has been inhabited.

Perhaps. Space probes sent to the red planet are looking for signs of life. We shall soon know the answer.

True o

Fake medicines can heal.

True. Thanks to the placebo effect, you can heal ill people using totally useless medicines. Experience shows that fake injections are more effective than fake pills! How does this placebo effect work? Nobody really knows.

Scientists are not interested in imaginary animals.

False. Cryptozoologists are scientists who believe that a story of a make-believe animal may hide the existence of an unknown species. This was how giant squid were discovered, on which sperm whales feed more than 1,000 m deep in the sea.

The mystery of the disappearance of the dinosaurs has at last been solved.

True. It happened after an enormous meteorite landed, producing a cloud of dust that obscured the atmosphere and prevented plants from growing, and herbivores from eating. The impact of the shock has been discovered in the Gulf of Mexico.

At Lourdes, ill people are 'miraculously' healed.

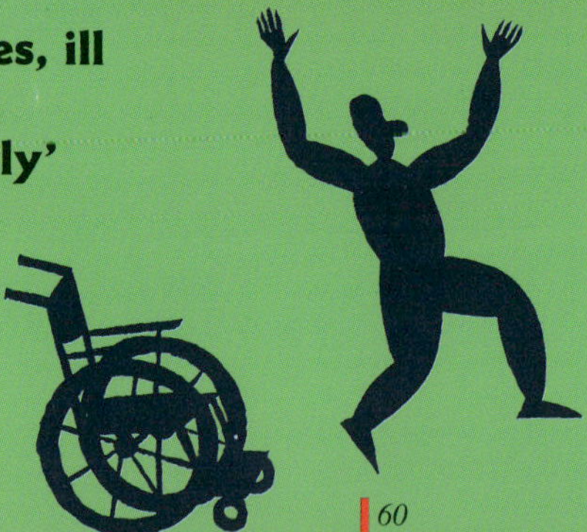

Perhaps. Some pilgrims with strong beliefs have been inexplicably healed of incurable diseases. But have miracles really taken place?

False?

A plane has been invented that can detect the existence of oil.

False. In 1978, the story of sniffer planes was an enormous hoax that cost the ELF oil company millions of francs.

Science and religion are rivals.

False. Science seeks to explain how the world functions, whereas religion is more concerned with why we exist on Earth.

The Seven Wonders of the World have all been destroyed.

False. While the Hanging Gardens of Babylon, the Lighthouse of Alexandria, the Colossus of Rhodes, the Temple of Artemis at Ephesus, the statue of Zeus at Olympia and the Mausoleum at Halicarnassus have all been destroyed, the Egyptian pyramids are still standing.

The Romans transported standing stones weighing more than 800 tonnes.

True. Three of them make up part of the Baalbeck Temple in Lebanon (20 m long, 4 m wide and 4 m high).

Index

Solution to the game on pages 26-27

You should have found the make-up artist's feather duster, the two moons, the witch's broom the wrong way round, the camera the wrong way round, the director's funnel, the carrot at the end of the microphone, the sound engineer's stethoscope, the sound box unconnected, the man stabbed with a sword, the woman with her bust the wrong way round, the carnivorous plant eating a telephone, the picture of a vampire with a cross round its neck, the ghost dressed in patterned material, the decapitated person, the dog with two heads, the man walking on the wall, the portrait without a face, the owl with a pig in its claws, the torch supported by a foot, the escalator, the horseman wearing a cosmonaut's helmet, the secret passage.

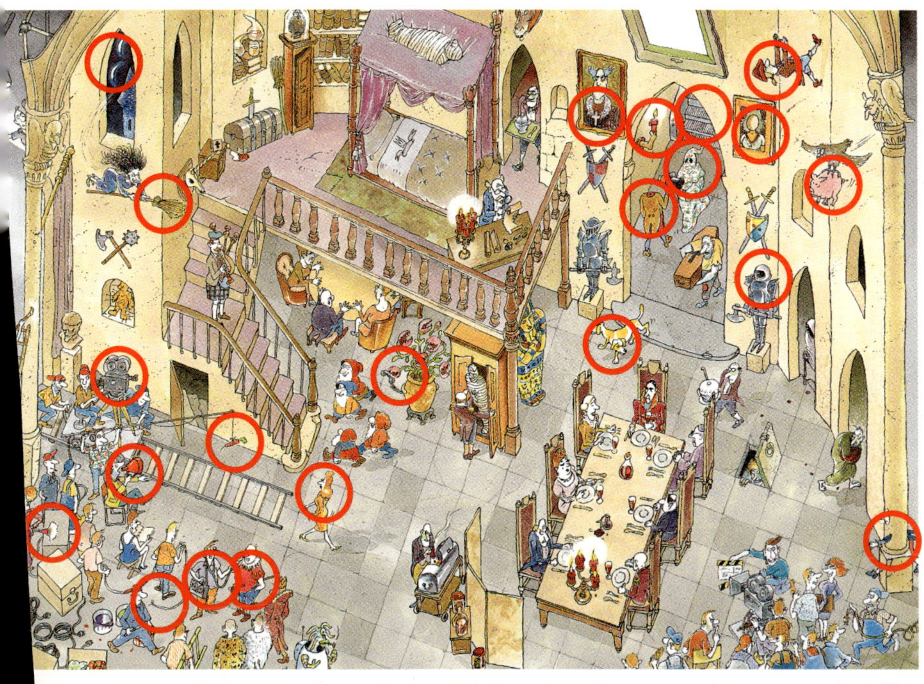

Created by Marie-Odile Fordacq
Authors François Aulas, Herbert Ben Kemoun, Béatrice Garel, Catherine Pauwels
Managing editors Marie-Odile Fordacq, Camilla Hallinan
Editorial co-ordinators Ariane Léandri, Molly Perham
Art editors Sue Aldworth, Ch'en Ling, Bernard Girodroux, Val Pidgeon
Illustrators Ian Chamberlain, Izhar Cohen, Elaine Cox, Mark Edwards, Jeff Fisher, Daniel Guerrier, Nick Hall, Michael Johnson, Louise Kelly, Robert Mason, Danuta Mayer, Tony McSweeney, Caroline Thomson, Richard Ward, Andrew Wheatcroft
Activities Ting Morris, Tim Ridley Photography, Val Wright
Photo research Veneta Bullen
Photo credits AKG London, Fortean Picture Library, Griffith Institute (Ashmolean Museum Oxford), Images Colour Library, Kobal Collection, Moulinsart Brussels
Design and page make-up équipage, Olivier Lemoine, Judy Linard, Terry Woodley

KINGFISHER
An imprint of Kingfisher Publications Plc
New Penderel House, 283–288 High Holborn, London WC1V 7HZ

This edition first published by Kingfisher Publications Plc 1998
Originally published in France by Nathan
under the title *Megascope: Vrais et faux mystères du monde*

2 4 6 8 10 9 7 5 3 1

A CIP catalogue record for this book is available from the British Library

ISBN 07534 0 221 1

Printed in Italy

Stickers

The kiss of the vampire
(Isabelle Adjani and Klaus Kinski, 1978)

The film *Ghostbusters* introduced some ve
badly brought up ghosts.

Seen in Spring, the little fairy Primevera brings happiness.

An Indian fakir